THE NATURE KIDS GUIDE TO
FENNEC FOXES

DAVID ANDERSON

For information address LP Media Inc. Publishing,
30012 Variolite St NW, Princeton MN 55371
www.lpmedia.org

Publication Data

Fennec Foxes
The Nature Kid's Guide to Fennec Foxes — First edition.

Summary: "Learn all about Fennec Foxes, the Nature Kid Way"
— Provided by publisher.

ISBN: 979-8-89818-136-9

[1. Fennec Foxes – Non-Fiction] I. Title.

Title: The Nature Kid's Guide to Fennec Foxes

CONTENTS

SAND LIFE

The Sahara Desert gets very little rain, less than one inch per year! Fennec foxes get most of their water from the food they eat.

Yip! A small fox peeks out from its sandy burrow. Its big ears twitch.

Fennec foxes live in some of the hottest places on Earth. The sand can get hot enough to burn your skin during the day. But fennec foxes have clever ways to survive here.

These foxes make their homes underground. They dig burrows in the sand that stay cool even when it is hot outside.

Fennec foxes rest in their dens during the day. The desert heat does not bother them there. At night, the sand cools down. That is when these foxes come out to explore.

DESERT DWELLERS

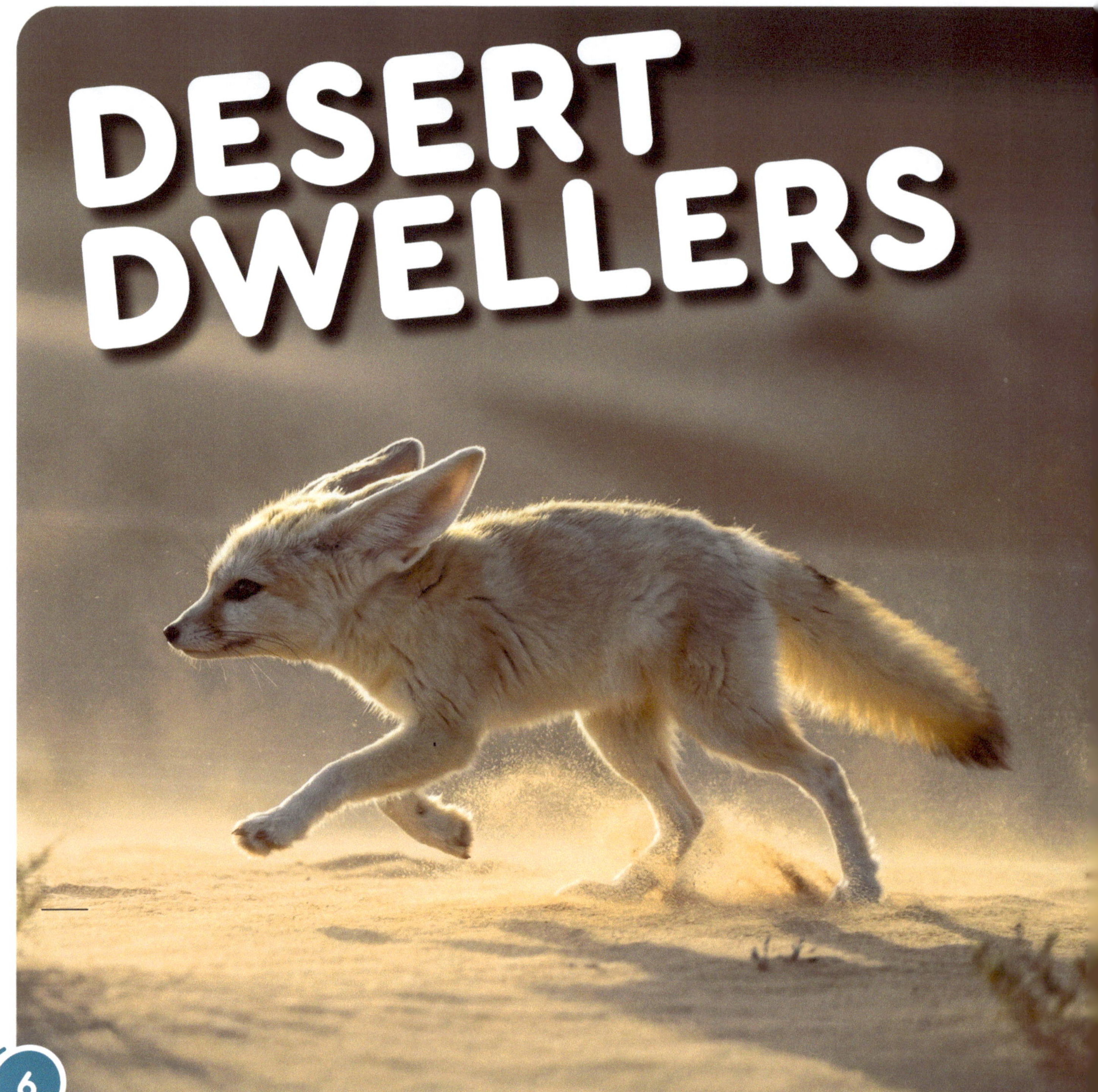

Whoosh! Wind blows sand. A small fox runs through dust.

Fennec foxes live in North Africa. They roam the Sahara Desert. They live in dry lands too.

You can find them in countries like Morocco, Egypt, and Sudan.

These foxes like living in sandy deserts. They need loose soil to dig their **burrows**.

Fennec foxes do not live anywhere else. They are true desert animals.

The Sahara Desert is huge! It is almost as big as the entire United States.

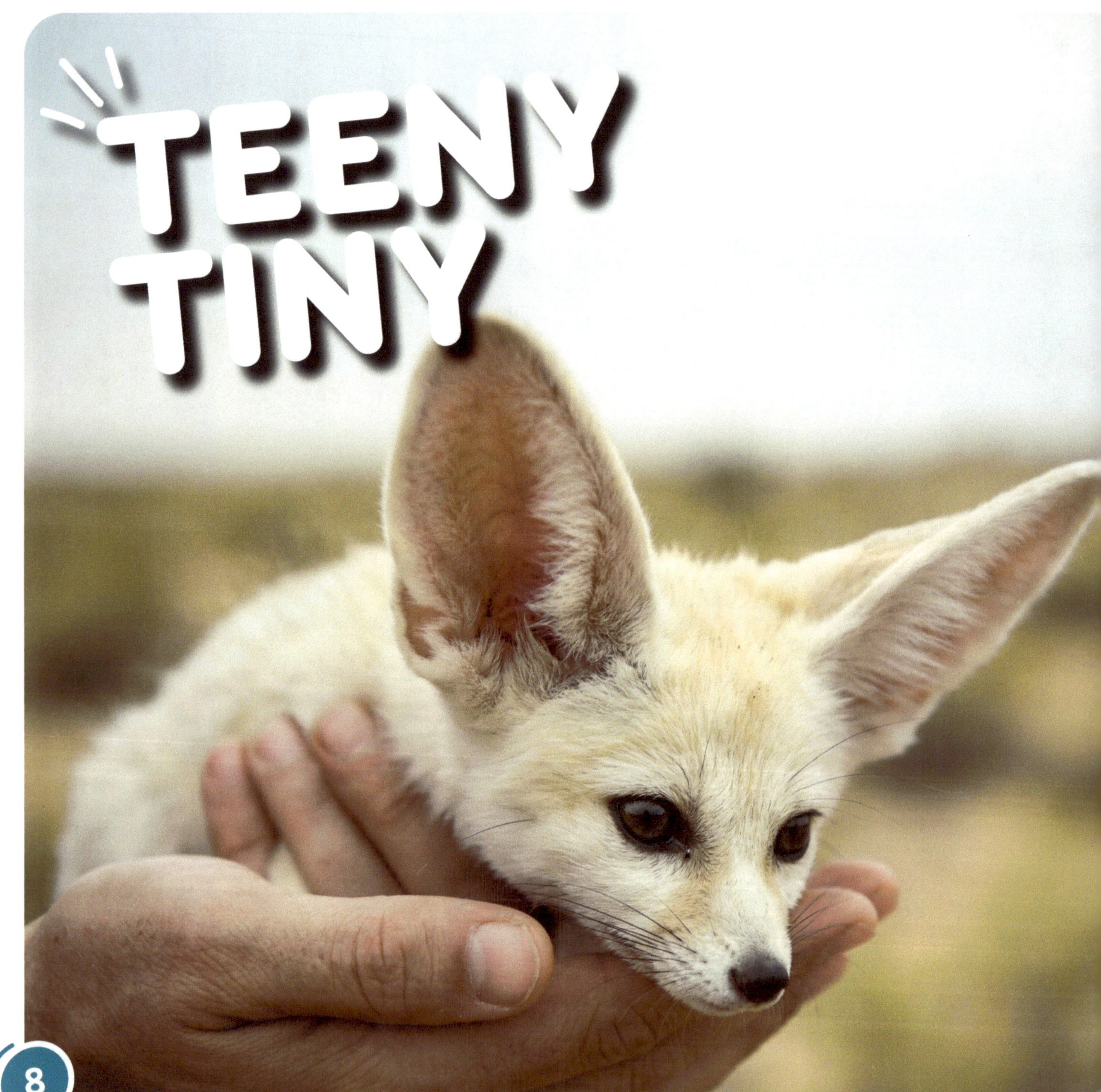

TEENY
TINY

Squeak! A tiny fox sits in a person's cupped hands.

Fennec foxes are the smallest foxes in the world. They weigh only 2 to 3 pounds. That is about half as big as the average cat!

A fennec fox is about 9 to 16 inches long. Its bushy tail adds another 7 to 12 inches.

Their soft fur has two layers. A fluffy undercoat keeps them warm on cold desert nights. The outer coat reflects the hot sun. Even the bottoms of their paws are covered in thick fur. This keeps their feet safe on the hot desert sand.

A fennec fox could stand on this book! Its paws are only about one inch wide.

ENORMOUS EARS

Twitch! A fennec fox turns its huge ears. It listens closely.

Fennec foxes have very big ears. No other fox has ears this big for its body size. Their ears can grow up to 6 inches long. That is almost half the size of their whole body!

Those big ears help fennec foxes stay cool. Blood flows through the thin skin. The heat leaves through their ears.

The ears also help them hear tiny sounds. They can even hear a beetle crawling under the sand.

Fennec foxes can turn each ear a different way at the same time!

SUPER SENSES

Sniff! A fennec fox smells a tiny bug under the sand.

Fennec foxes have great senses. Their eyes work well in the dark. A special layer in their eyes bounces light back in. This helps them see when hunting at night. It also makes their eyes glow!

Fennec foxes have a great sense of smell too. They press their nose to the sand to sniff out bugs and lizards hiding below. Then they dig with all four paws to catch their meal.

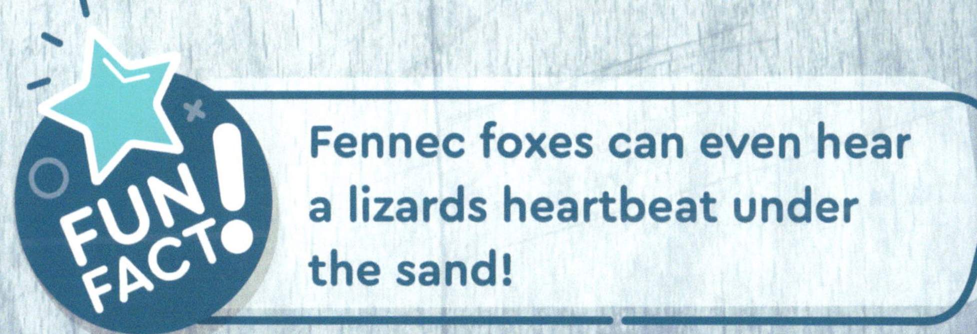

BLENDING IN

Shhh! A fennec fox hides in the sand. Can you see it?

Fennec foxes have sandy-colored fur. This pale cream color matches the desert around them. Predators have a hard time spotting them!

Their fur blends with rocks and sand dunes. When a fennec fox stays still, it almost disappears. This is called **camouflage**.

Even their belly fur is light colored. This helps them hide when lying flat on warm sand.

A fennec fox's fur also reflects sunlight. This keeps the fox cooler during hot days.

15

FENNEC FOODS

Crunch! A fennec fox bites a beetle. Yum!

Fennec foxes eat over 400 types of food. They munch on insects. They eat lizards. They catch small rodents. They also eat bird eggs.

These little foxes like plants too. They nibble on roots. They eat fruits and berries. Desert plants give them water.

Fennec foxes get most of their water from food. This helps them live in the dry desert where water is hard to find.

Fennec foxes bury extra food in sand. They save it to eat as a tasty treat later!

POUNCE POWER
FUN FACT!
Fennec foxes can dig through sand in seconds to catch buried insects and lizards.
18

Pounce! A fennec fox leaps high into the air and dives headfirst!

Fennec foxes are skilled hunters. They use a special move called **pouncing**. The fox jumps up and lands on prey with its front paws.

They listen carefully before they pounce. Their big ears help them know exactly where prey hides. Then they leap up to 2 feet in the air!

Fennec foxes hunt alone at night. They walk slowly and quietly across the sand.

When they hear their prey moving, they strike fast. One quick pounce catches dinner.

DANGER LURKS

Screech! A large eagle swoops down from the sky. A fennec fox runs!

Fennec foxes face many dangers. Eagles and owls hunt them from above. These big birds have sharp eyes and talons.

Jackals and hyenas also hunt fennec foxes. These **predators** roam the desert looking for food. They can smell a fox from far away.

Even some snakes are dangerous. Horned vipers hide under the sand. Fennec foxes must always stay alert to survive.

Eagle owls can spot prey from miles away! Their huge eyes help them hunt.

DIG DEEP

Dig! A fennec fox kicks sand. Watch how fast it digs!

Fennec foxes dig very well. They use their paws like shovels. They move sand fast. A fennec fox can dig a burrow 32 feet long!

Burrows keep fennec foxes safe. When danger comes, they run underground. Eagles cannot follow them. Jackals cannot follow them either.

Burrows stay cool on hot days. Fennec foxes rest inside. They wait until night.

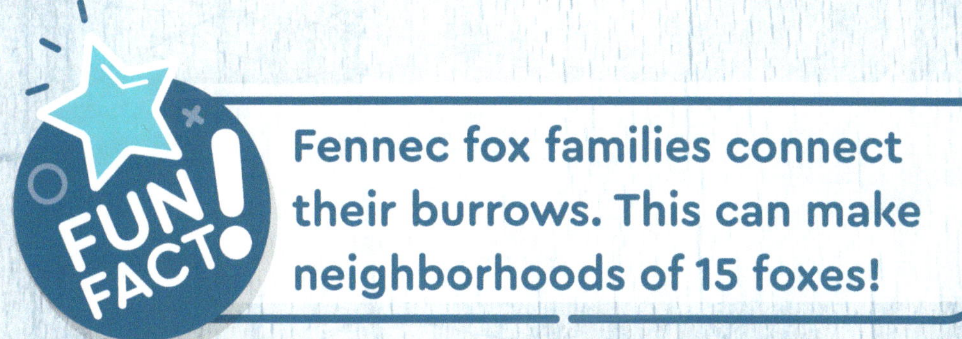

FAST FEET

Swoosh! A fennec fox zooms across the sand. Its small legs move fast!

Fennec foxes are quick runners. They can sprint up to 20 miles per hour. That is faster than most people can run!

Their small, light bodies help them move fast.

They are also very agile. They can twist and turn quickly to escape predators like jackals. Their bushy tails help them steer!

Speedy hunting dogs chase fennec foxes in the desert. But the foxes twist and turn so fast that the dogs hardly ever catch them!

NIGHT SHIFT

Hoot! The sun sets. A fennec fox wakes up in the desert.

Fennec foxes are **nocturnal**. This means they are active at night. They sleep during the hot day.

Night is much cooler in the desert. It can drop 50 degrees after sunset.

Fennec foxes hunt at night in the cooler weather. Many desert bugs and rodents come out at night too. The foxes and their prey are all active at the same time!

Fennec foxes are most active right after sunset. Their prey is just waking up then. This makes it easy to catch!

FOXES
TOGETHER

Bark! Three fennec foxes come out of their burrow. They live together!

Fennec foxes live in family groups. A group can have up to 10 foxes. They share one big burrow.

Family members groom each other. They play together at night. Young foxes wrestle. They chase their siblings.

Fennec foxes make many sounds. They bark. They whine. They purr. Each sound means something different.

Fennec fox families mark their home with scent. This tells other foxes to stay away!

FINDING MATES

Howl! A fennec fox calls out in the dark. Another fox answers!

Fennec foxes form pairs. A male and female stay together to mate. They can be partners for life.

Males mark their land with scent. They also bring food to females. They do this before the pair has babies.

Fennec foxes mate between January and March. Desert nights are cooler then. This timing helps keep baby foxes safe.

Fennec foxes can have up to 5 babies at once. Most pairs have 2 to 4 kits each year.

FUZZY KITS

Fennec fox kits are born with downy white fur. Their fur turns sandy tan as they grow older.

Purr! Fuzzy fennec kits snuggle in their cozy den.

Baby fennec foxes are called kits. A mother usually has two to five kits at once. Each newborn weighs only about 1.5 ounces.

Kits are born with their eyes closed. Their eyes open after about ten days. Their famous big ears are floppy at first too.

Kits drink their mother's milk for the first weeks. Then they start eating solid food around five weeks old. By three months, young foxes look like small adults.

FAMILY FIRST

Bark! A father fox brings food to his den. His family waits inside.

Fennec fox parents work together to raise their kits. The father protects the den and the family. He also hunts and brings back food.

The mother stays close to her babies. She keeps them warm and fed. Both parents protect their young from danger.

Kits often stay with their family for a year or more. During this time, they learn important skills.

DID YOU KNOW?

Fennec fox kits learn to hunt by pouncing on siblings during play!

DESERT PROS

Thump! A fennec fox taps the cool sand with its paw.

Fennec foxes have a neat trick for staying cool. They pant! When the desert gets very hot, they breathe super fast.

A resting fox takes about 23 breaths per minute. But a hot fox can take 690 breaths per minute! That is 30 times faster. All that fast breathing lets heat escape from their body.

When desert nights get cold, fennec foxes shiver to warm up. Their bodies work hard to handle both hot and cold!

Fennec foxes huge ears can let out extra heat to cool them down!

FOX
SPOTTING

Click! A camera snaps a photo. A fennec fox looks up.

You do not have to travel to Africa to see a fennec fox. Many zoos and wildlife centers have them!

Look for them in small mammal houses. They may be curled up sleeping during your visit. That is because they are nocturnal.

Ask a zookeeper about fennec foxes. They love to share fun facts! You might even see the foxes wake up near closing time.

Some wildlife watchers use red lights to see fennec foxes. Red light does not scare them away!

GLOSSARY

burrow
A hole or tunnel that an animal digs in the ground to live in.

predators
Animals that hunt and eat other animals.

nocturnal
An animal that sleeps during the day and is awake at night.

camouflage
Colors or patterns that help an animal hide by matching what is around it.

pouncing
Jumping up and landing on something to catch it.